HOURGLASS STUDIES

Krysia Jopek

HOURGLASS STUDIES

Poems ©2017 by Krysia Jopek
krysiajopek.com
all rights reserved by the author

Cover design by Dale Houstman
facebook.com/dalehoustman

Crisis Chronicles #95
ISBN: 978-1-940996-46-2
1st edition, 2nd printing

Published 31 October 2017 by
Crisis Chronicles Press
3431 George Avenue
Parma, Ohio 44134 USA

crisischronicles.com
ccpress.blogspot.com
facebook.com/crisischroniclespress

With every line one broke off a bit of the world

—*Rainer Maria Rilke*

I

1. A clock points the exit of bliss balanced with the least severe bitterness. To want so much and turn over pliant grains of sand without meaning.

2. Lurking at the windows, unfrequented by time's defiant passing, a lying [still], a counting down.

3. Following the Jesus-loving holy, the carpet stolen from the forest wrapped into a shawl, growing tall, heavy eyelids tugged— uphill.

4. Dragons apple green set the toy ships free, decoys to track the [im]possible.

5. What cannot be told in the usual way, cannot be placed in parentheses [*Winter*].

6. When the train stalls the homeless cornered, the boy with white columbines in his arms. Reason[s] won't jump up to be claimed properly.

7. One scrapes the bone for flesh, mea[n]t to flavor the broth, trailing the flanks of snails, cells for the slide, a figure to draw and study as if familiar.

8. Holes need laughter because sadness s[wall]ows the meadow that needs to drink the sun.

9. Reflecting abandoned cities, the train flows past. A mathematical problem deferred [like [an] Echo].

10. Segues of [slip]pages, nightmares buried beneath the boathouse, coalescing scenes, torn pocket, cup of win[e], more than could be planned.

11. Those story-facts, dust of the empirical, collage spun into pastiche by emphatic critics stripping the coda. Everything reified; *go home.*

12. Up against the lightning-struck tree, a sharded pill[ar] receding, view new, slipping real, the words in the book, a blur.

II

1. The barnyard rotten and hollowed; termites eating away at the grotesque. Nothing planned [could be] recompense, everything lost, buried alive.

2. The beginning lifts the plane off the ground, but where to go at high speed gliding?

3. The marbled notebook connects as many points as possible: a dilapidated figure, flailing constellation, door that leads out of one complicated situation into another. . .

4. The interpretation, a tango with the pieces, skating under the house that has moved the abacus [*abscess*].

5. Here for listening, reconstructing the intricate threshold, therapy or boredom, the three-year-old already in need of new toys.

6. A week is too long to be running in the same direction, pulled back to go further. *Hurry up so we can relax, go!*

7. Keys flung from pockets, the knapsack of questions dumped on the kitchen table with a severity that knows no law. An antinomian feat.

8. The time clock shall forgive, the papers will not miss [us], the hurt bird will soon focus, forget us.

9. A landscape not even imagined spills onto the painter's toes. Caused by a conglomeration of consequences, pieced together much later with the deadening, sleepless fact[s].

10. The division is actually useful; be glad.

11. Particles spin and spin but stay in place [some]how.

12. The signpost [D]ANGER, stitching the surface, swimming in open spaces, treading circuitous repetitions: *want*[*ing*] *too* [*little too*] *intensely carrying nowhere* [*still*].

III

1. History repeats itself and forgets the neighbors who watch TV twenty-four hours a day, the daughter who never goes to sleep, plodding the interstices of commercials.

2. Daylight, desire, and apathy hold hands. For $30 the truck will come and suck out the autumn leaves. Round out the figures and throw the tallies away.

3. The cleaning woman will find the grandmother's broach, the Japanese dragon chasing its tail, and the child will lose it again. *Stubborn pigeons under the eaves.*

4. With enough discipline one could get used to the killings in the road, the public space gone poor.

5. Suburbs envelope the dump of trees planted by Republicans to illustrate they grow. [A *post*-humanist party can't afford a party outdoors on TV.]

6. Make art, not babies, maybe one, screaming in the post office, tearing all the trees down.

7. When what is wanted is presented to satiate those unspeakable cravings, remember the Three Graces [poised alabaster], the way one wants the lighting filled in.

8. Spit back   the littered   streets   often grow [*violas*].

9. A poetics can be given, poorly explained, summarized only at one point: a permanent transition, a steady fraction-glimpse, delicately spun.

10. To downscale unscales the number of complicated forms.

11. The news predicted changes that carry no guarantee, for the company folded after illustrating what to buy, wish for secretly— reflected *ad infinitum* on the mass media screen: tablets to take away hunger, new perfume [*Compunction*], dependable insurance, lucky numbers, the ability to catch on.

12. The weather person assures there will be other beautiful days, stuporous with transience, impinging a darkness folded within, something [we've] never wanted to be a part of, that same cloth.

IV

1. The relationship among objects, a [meta]physical calculation. A hand wants a shadow.

2. When you put your finger on the word [*balustrade*], the hand[le] slips out of focus, displaces the current.

3. Going somewhere this time [we are] certain of the angle of the horizon, how to end the ungodly routine.

4. To lament character, a waste of expenditure. Announcing a new itinerary, the inventory signed, one last sigh for putting things on their shelves, tidy, [un]locked.

5. One is alone, but secretly glad, when the pink sky calls [*red*].

6. To talk in abstractions, doesn't amount to anything at the end of a column; the last day of a vacation around the [*is*]land, different each time.

7. When they embark there would be sightings: tools ready, knives sharpened after dark.

8. Three thousand [birds] chant the temple [remarkable collection, witness, provisional split] a dualism of [syn]tax, duplicitous triumphs, the simplification of complexity, the necessary ablation.

9. The lantern from Egypt pulled from the window by the storm's backhand.

10. A spiritual moment: to forget and remember and forget what was forgotten and be surprised and remember [again]. . . the distance from _____, the subtraction involved.

11. A country of temples roped off   the queen of light
a broken doll   husk   sheathing   abstract   particulars.

12. To inscribe an ideal would devalue the *rest*, a dusting of gladness in the turret, a lightness full-lipped, clothed in winds [wings] of drapery.

V

1. Autumn carries winter in her lap, Orpheo looking back for a one-act reckoning to decorate   shifting   spheres.

2. So many choices, glosses, ways of seeing   invisible   coat-strings weighing down.

3. Vitriolic images unfold sound, impinged fractions pierce tiny welcome.

4. With each piece of evidence, the outcome purported, existential information to appease the most stubborn philosophers, oblivious to the demands of Monday [unable to tie one shoe].

5. Hibernation promised for the skeleton laying down unattended, separated from history.

6. Someone convinces we were needed in that house where sorrow slips in on a Saturday, accordions the stairs.

7. The voices of children coming home from school coax a language of follow. *A curriculum of cymbals.*

8. One dead white bird disintegrates on the pavement and is not a metaphor. Nor a quantity [*echo*].

9. The boy knew his multiplication tables up to nine.

10. We'll miss your furrowed forehead, moon, your delicate paper maché.

11. *Yes, I raised pigeons in black and white where the river missed _____; please have lunch without.*

12. Tell the girl she'll need more armor; kindness a cloud—her hair, a pillow-curse.

VI

1. Nasturtium trumpets, faded goldfish, tumble down and *chaos* becomes a favorite word in the house where entropy refracts company.

2. Autumn crumpled into a paper ball unfolded in candlelight impatiently: *The gardeners are tired and dream of winter.*

3. The forearm tied with russet [silk] gives in to grammar, the *porch of lighthouse-gather.*

4. Poetic words: trees to hide between: changing time: chopped down: not timing the future, upcoming   bend.

5. The watch buried in the sewer, forgetting the way to go there to say. *Car horns pierce Thursday with hurry. The outline of the [human] [subject] can't be excised.*

6. Experiment in poetry means. . .

7. To rhyme would give credence, an echo to resound through time; the stone skipped back through the river.

8. Disappearing but moving, the train receding, haunts afternoons with a crash. The sleeper in slow motion approaching [the] sublime.

9. The puppeteer's drunk fingers [undoing _____], too heavy with fright.

10. The other turn led through the abandoned garden because of no one's fault. The drought caused those tired to move on *because the gardener loved bones.*

11. Abstract persona [anonymous] eating *ennui.*

12. Wrists ache for a paintbrush to supersede the photograph. Neck falls to confound interval, whispers to the knees to straighten and heal, forget the long winter up ahead.

VII

1. Every night from the subway the clock's dark hands pointing to locate a portion of the whole and make it recurrent, [re]marked.

2. A variation of the same variables.

3. Names can be changed, change can be given, wind can push light objects through the street.

4. If the snow would come as the almanac promised, perhaps the illusion of starting over, keeping the record clean, all of those dark marks [re]moved.

5. Tongues purified, the worst memories recede temporarily: a sudden turning: undefiant nominalism: a skirting of the issue.

6. Sacrifice calls the negation of desire, postponement of the infinite. *The crack vials were hidden. I did touch you but I froze.*

7. Unsure footsteps on the pavement promise a stranger carrying a silver tray of moon. [He is late but there is no other, and to assume so undercuts his bounty].

8. The smile signed mischievously, as if an El Greco or a life of *pure poetry*.

9. Repeatedly, expectations swept out of the house: the prince-madrigal kindness, *use before dark*. Fire escapes ready, numbers posted in case of emergency.

10. The elephant glowing, assembled for the sick child alone at the escarpment.

11. To eradicate the sickness pull up from the roots, coddle in an uncompromising way. The fragmented parable instills value of the [im]material, green dust in fingertips.

12. Orpheo at the cliffs gathers the ruffles of sun. Torrential downpour and thunder [deco]rate sleep to tell of the [s]hip, the [t]rain, the waiting to be carried [a book] under someone's arm.

VIII

1. What is wished has dire beckonings. The Bedouins move in. There is no method to explain that funk.

2. Misled through careless wreckage, the fools play dead.

3. Because of all those movies, they came here, fumbled. To be fully on guard; appendages, functional.

4. Alabaster women with seaweed hair watch over because someone wanted some form of begin.

5. Racing his new bike, the boy pleads for *infinity, dreaming pipe dreams*, his father's thick hands grasping him at the collar.

6. The *good* boy in the fable broke his leg and had to stay in the castle for many days; his best friend staring at him from across the shore soon forgets. *Solitude overwhelming, the sea's steady voice*.

7. Curious at the old cemetery, a whole set of problems can't be etched into the tree's thick trunk, transcribed with linen paper; side to side, skipping backwards through the hurricane.

8. The bus of strangers passes   achingly   somehow familiar resembling those missed most in sleep.

9. One and another joined by a rusted hinge, like an object, subjected to scrutiny: a forensic investigation replete with graph-paper crib sheets, *wake up, be alert but not too nervous the time will be up, nowhere to go.*

10. Energy and dissipation [acedia's dissertation] undo eternity's fence. To be near another is no guarantor.

11. We are happier ever since they took the BMW away. No third party is needed for the argument that cannot be proven outside of the set.

12. Time remains one-sided. All winter the gardener weeps under ice.

IX

1. Dawn fingers an invisible mathematician. The sage peering into a handful of burnt leaves.

2. *Make a bed for the voyagers, a canopy that tucks away impervious [dawn], Odysseus kissing the [ground].*

3. As if understanding the deepest of things casually, a girl twirls her Botticelli hair. *Was it a real betrayal if it wasn't planned?*

4. There wasn't time to get drunk, say what we really thought stopped in its trajectory, on course.

5. *Of course* you say *I am listening*, but are filled with sleep, carrying baskets of pears into other lands.

6. All the dominos fell and left no one standing. How to recognize _____ after paying such tolls?
   [ourselves]

7. The did done poorly, the bone hinged back unbroken, the thing thrown, the night a bent boomerang that comes back for no reason, no pretty string of nacreous beads.

8. The tests cost too much money to flirt with frivolity's new lipstick. Say *I refuse to paint by numbers, count the holes in the ceiling, evil thoughts on my toes*, telling the dog afraid of snow to go.

9. So many years in the attic, the cartography faded [;] without a small pair of hands to touch the arteries, the leaf of the metropolis shorn.

10. Magnetized to the floor, the character cannot arise from the death scene, forgotten by everyone else on stage. The audience already went home and dug cathartic holes.

11. There was no getting nearer or counting that far. The bottle of medicine broke. *I licked the ground and fell back, a war*[*rior*] *against the many who stayed home half-heartedly.*

12. *Watching myself on a movie screen   I am awkward   ready to speak.*

X

1. Sentences drag luminous   solitudes   into the sea at dawn dislocating _____.

2. Luting the gap's fomentation, [the hours necessary but not constant], statement to hold as steadying branch.

3. The book of answers burns in the crossover of the baton as if one person could not be trusted. *I had everything to give until you started taking the sea from my ear to tell me I heard nothing.*

4. Sorrow in the toothbrush [al]located at birth. Remove the problematic gene and pass out pain[t] for everyone.

5. True or false: the *turtledove* related to a *moonflower*?

6. The goodbye proven with [photo]graphs, waiting for the roof to heal, undo the laces, finish the prop[hecy], so there could be surprise again *without the ego's shallow pit[fall]*.

7. Furiously night after night [p]urging emotions.

8. The poem wanted to be a city or a room where mus[ic] spills under the [do][or]. A difficult juggling recorded by the architect's steady [h]and.

9. A new philosophy pinned down in object-abstractions invested with atonal song.

10. The notebook [of winter] fell from the wind[ow]. Everything heavy when days are X-rayed by night, the chest falls back [in c]loud.

11. Pleading for a speedy recovery, extended hospitality, the clown plays an accordion while crying to make extra money. Another comes to title the composition [*Melanc*]*holy*.

12. The storm hits recklessly and one forgets which words. . .an object, a branch of [st]rings. Who can jump from the highest? The feet sting upon landing: memory [g]losses ambit[ion].

XI

1. Sleeping close to the reef, the traveler holds a teal cup to the ear to hear the blue-green kelp gone lazy and dry, lost from the ink [stomach].

2. The chair in the suitcase packed to find the third shore, [w]here another narration varies.

3. In the dirt lit with Chinatown, the refrain apprehended in part; the loss of the second hand.

4. Send for the sample only to be plagued by more questionnaires.

5. The contents of the bag turned inside out. Borrowed and given back: a loose tooth, address book, bit of red mountain in a jar.

6. The lover's eye   spinning   estuary   coin.

7. Pulled out of slumber across the daybook filled to echo formulas for [sw]allowed halos.

8. The clock in hand   the confused woman swallows the key to a diary   the pages disappear   waiting for the trump finale.

9. The [n]arrow boatride   toward   daybreak
before   the mountains   crumbled   [into]   sound.

10. Pendulum's dialectic of *true* and *false*, and all those shades of gray in between conspire hungry.

11. To prove the best design, the tincture couldn't be documented to ensure the singular.

12. The hemlock given with an even hand, the logician attacked in the folds of a proposition, knotted in the tide's undercurrent, wakes to find everyone missing—all of the main beams.

XII

1. Hungry for orientation: up one street, turn back, then another abandoned parking lot, house overgrown with chestnut trees, flights of stairs [that] lead to a better view [vertigo], dim river rippled with oil, blackbirds at impeccable attention.

2. A glass case with a thousand clocks, each with a different face and placement of arms. The watch keeper perpetually dusting and shifting them around to confuse or stay busy.

3. The hourglass flipped the conversation over. How to end when one doesn't recognize the beginning?

4. *I wake and remember I am [a] stranger   egregiously misled. Tomorrow I shall forget   depart through the back porch with stolen photographs.*

5. The Green Clowns sleeping; the poet spinning cream-page tangos on the balcony—perfunctory.

6. *Being what they seem*, pulling the threads, making up what they mean without verbal irony, they have arrived on time; time again has meaning.

7. How many mirrors refract the whole story, how many know the truth?

8. *Push me!* The boy orders   the swing   tangling verdant [lush]   decrescendo[s] [of] the marshland   arching   from the definitive.

9. The director's arms rock the camera and eucalyptus drunkenly
and [time] becomes a [char]acter.

10. The boy will dream of sharks and tell another in sleep: the ocean too dark to know

11. [if space is hollow or open].

12. Beauty and terror, paper-chain cartwheels spin hour over hour, up through the [sentence] structure, *being*, strange window.

Acknowledgments

Selections from *HOURGLASS STUDIES* debuted online in *Meta/Phor(e) /Play*.

The Rilke epigraph comes from *The Notebooks of Malte Lourids Brigge*, translated by M.D. Herter Norton.